Remember When...?

Remember geometric hair cuts and trickle-down economics?
How about Mary Lou Retton, or Duran Duran?
Can you remember when Yuppies were common,
or when the novels of Stephen King were uncommonly cool?

Then you must be ready for a 80s party!

THIS BOOK OF MEMORIES PRESENTED TO:

_____

ON THE OCCASION OF:

_____

DATE:

SETTING THE SCENE

1980
- Mt. St. Helens erupts in Washington state
- John Lennon is gunned down in front of his apartment building by a deranged fan
- Billionaire Ted Turner launches CNN, the first channel devoted to round-the-clock news
- E-mail spreads in the US thanks to the acceptance of the Internet

1981
- MTV begins broadcasting
- Diana Spencer weds England's Prince Charles
- AIDS is officially recognized by the US government
- Sandra Day O'Connor is the first woman to be named to the US Supreme Court
- American Airlines introduces a frequent flyer program
- President Reagan is shot and seriously wounded by John Hinckley Jr

1982
- *USA Today* begins publication
- The Vietnam Veterans Memorial is dedicated in Washington, D.C.
- Tylenol is recalled nationwide when cyanide-laced capsules kill seven people in Chicago
- Barney Clark receives the first permanent artificial heart implant; he survives for 112 days
- Disney opens EPCOT Center in Florida

1983
- Karen Carpenter, aged 32, dies of a heart attack brought on by anorexia
- Sally K. Ride becomes the first American female astronaut to enter outer space
- Vanessa Williams is the first black woman to become Miss America
- The Trivial Pursuit board game becomes an instant hit
- The first cellular phone network is inaugurated in Chicago by AT&T

1984
- HIV is identified as the cause of AIDS
- DNA sequencing is developed by scientist Alec Jeffreys
- Apple introduces the first Macintosh

1985
- Coca-Cola® introduces New Coke®; it lasts just ten weeks
- Forty-five rock, pop and country stars record "We Are the World" to call attention to African famine victims
- The first Farm Aid concert—to benefit farmers at risk of foreclosure—is organized by singer Willie Nelson

1986
- Bill Gates takes Microsoft public, and becomes an instant millionaire
- The space shuttle Challenger explodes 73 seconds after liftoff, killing all seven aboard
- Martin Luther King Jr.'s birthday becomes a national holiday
- England's Prince Andrew marries Sarah Ferguson

1987 · Televangelist Jim Bakker reveals that he committed adultery and stole from his ministry
· Presidential hopeful Gary Hart withdraws after being photographed with a woman other than his wife

1988 · Pan Am Flight 103 explodes over Lockerbie, Scotland, killing all 259 aboard
· Used needles and vials of blood wash up on the shore of Long Island

1989 · An earthquake strikes northern California, doing enormous damage in the San Francisco Bay area
· The Communist East German government collapses, and with it, the Berlin Wall
· Hurricane Hugo destroys the coast of the Carolinas, causing $4 billion in damage
· The oil tanker Exxon Valdez runs aground in Alaska, spilling over ten million gallons of crude oil

The Buzz

Toxic shock syndrome

Robert Mapplethorpe

Jimmy Swaggart

KAL 007   The Mouth from the South

cocaine

Baby M   Jean Harris

Wayne B. Williams

The Teflon president

Greed is good

Where's the beef?

Trickle-down economics

Donna Rice   New Coke®

Tammy Faye   Jelly Bellies®

California Raisins   Lee Iacocca

Claymation   The Great Communicator

Donald Trump   Yuppies

MBA

Surrogate mother

Top of the Charts

♪ DON'T WORRY, BE HAPPY	Bobby McFerrin
♪ THRILLER	Michael Jackson
♪ LIKE A VIRGIN	Madonna
♪ GIRLS JUST WANT TO HAVE FUN	Cyndi Lauper
♪ LOVE SHACK	The B-52s
♪ WHO'S THAT GIRL	The Eurythmics
♪ THE WAY IT IS	Bruce Hornsby
♪ BORN IN THE U.S.A.	Bruce Springsteen
♪ HOW WILL I KNOW	Whitney Houston
♪ LADY	Kenny Rogers
♪ CALL ME	Blondie
♪ STARTING OVER	John Lennon
♪ ANOTHER BRICK IN THE WALL	Pink Floyd
♪ CRAZY LITTLE THING CALLED LOVE	Queen
♪ PHYSICAL	Olivia Newton-John
♪ BETTE DAVIS EYES	Kim Carnes
♪ ENDLESS LOVE	Diana Ross & Lionel Richie
♪ ARTHUR'S THEME	Christopher Cross
♪ KISS ON MY LIST	Daryl Hall & John Oates
♪ JESSIE'S GIRL	Rick Springfield
♪ EYE OF THE TIGER	Survivor
♪ CENTERFOLD	J. Geils Band
♪ MANEATER	Daryl Hall & John Oates
♪ JACK & DIANE	John Cougar
♪ I LOVE ROCK 'N' ROLL	Joan Jett and the Blackhearts
♪ EVERY BREATH YOU TAKE	Police
♪ FLASHDANCE	Irene Cara
♪ TOTAL ECLIPSE OF THE HEART	Bonnie Tyler
♪ DOWN UNDER	Men at Work
♪ WHEN DOVES CRY	Prince
♪ JUMP	Van Halen
♪ FOOTLOOSE	Kenny Loggins
♪ WHAT'S LOVE GOT TO DO WITH IT	Tina Turner
♪ I JUST CALLED TO SAY I LOVE YOU	Stevie Wonder
♪ GHOSTBUSTERS	Ray Parker Jr.
♪ KARMA CHAMELEON	Culture Club
♪ CAN'T FIGHT THIS FEELING	REO Speedwagon
♪ MONEY FOR NOTHING	Dire Straits
♪ SHOUT	Tears For Fears
♪ BROKEN WINGS	Mr. Mister
♪ I WANT TO KNOW WHAT LOVE IS	Foreigner
♪ THE POWER OF LOVE	Huey Lewis & the News
♪ WALK LIKE AN EGYPTIAN	Bangles
♪ FAITH	George Michael
♪ LIVIN' ON A PRAYER	Bon Jovi
♪ ROLL WITH IT	Steve Winwood
♪ NEVER GONNA GIVE YOU UP	Rick Astley
♪ STRAIGHT UP	Paula Abdul
♪ RIGHT HERE WAITING	Richard Marx
♪ ONE MORE NIGHT	Phil Collins
♪ UP WHERE WE BELONG	Joe Cocker and Jennifer Warnes

MUSIC

1980s

3

The Buzz

dance

the Ant
breakdancing
the Dolphin
moonwalk
the Bird
dirty dancing
Lambada
Funky Alien
the ska
Dancin' in the Dark
the Belinda

Devo

alternative

Guns n' Roses

Music video

Emmylou Harris

Young country

Julio Iglesias

Heavy metal

The Pretenders

New Age music

Milli Vanilli

Anita Baker

Hip hop

We Loved Our Television!

- ★ Dallas
- ★ ABC News Nightline
- ★ Magnum, P.I.
- ★ MTV
- ★ Dynasty
- ★ Hill Street Blues
- ★ Growing Pains
- ★ Family Ties
- ★ St. Elsewhere
- ★ Late Night with David Letterman
- ★ Cagney & Lacey
- ★ Remington Steele
- ★ Newhart
- ★ The A-Team
- ★ Night Court

- ★ Scarecrow & Mrs. King
- ★ The Bill Cosby Show
- ★ Miami Vice
- ★ Murder, She Wrote
- ★ Moonlighting
- ★ The Golden Girls
- ★ Cheers
- ★ L.A. Law
- ★ Spenser: For Hire
- ★ The Oprah Winfrey Show
- ★ Perfect Strangers
- ★ Alf
- ★ thirtysomething
- ★ Married...With Children
- ★ Beauty & the Beast
- ★ Murphy Brown

- ★ Roseanne
- ★ The Wonder Years
- ★ Wiseguy
- ★ The Arsenio Hall Show
- ★ Coach
- ★ China Beach

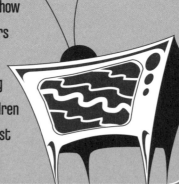

The Buzz

Who shot J.R.?
Ted Koppel
Max Headroom
The Huxtables
Let's be careful out there
Phil Donahue
Dr. Ruth
Stupid Pet Tricks

Whatever
Radical
Major
Way cool
Homeboy
Stoked
Cool beans
Get out
To the max
Yo!
Killer
Gross me out
Gag me with a spoon
Dude
Fer sure
No way
Awesome
Excellent
Bogus
Dork
Poser
As if
Elite
Stellar
Don't have a cow
Cool
Preppie
Heinous

Slang

TELEVISION

1980s

6

Movies We Had To See

Raging Bull
Coal Miner's Daughter
E.T.: The Extra-Terrestrial
On Golden Pond
Caddyshack
Sophie's Choice
Wall Street
Moonstruck
The Accused
My Left Foot
Dirty Dancing
The Big Chill
Back to the Future
Urban Cowboy

Risky Business
Flashdance
TRON
Tootsie
Batman
Ghostbusters
Top Gun
Lethal Weapon
Who Framed Roger Rabbit?
The Empire Strikes Back
Raiders of the Lost Ark
The Terminator
Die Hard
Fatal Attraction

Peggy Sue Got Married
An Officer and a Gentleman
A Nightmare on Elm Street
Three Men and a Baby
The Shining
Child's Play
Do the Right Thing
The Karate Kid
Airplane!
Ferris Bueller's Day Off
Bull Durham
Big
The Breakfast Club
Crocodile Dundee

Academy Award® Best Pictures

Robert De Niro

Sissy Spacek

John Hughes

Daniel Day-Lewis

Meryl Streep

The Brat Pack

Robert Duvall

Good Morning, Vietnam!

William Hurt

Shirley MacLaine

Sally Field

Marty McFly

Party on, dudes!

Eddie Murphy

Cher

Tom Cruise

Michael Douglas

Nicholas Cage

Molly Ringwald

Who ya gonna call?

The Buzz

MOVIES

1980s

8

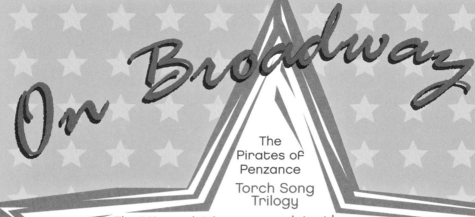

On Broadway

The Pirates of Penzance

Torch Song Trilogy

The Life and Adventures of Nicholas Nickleby

Into the Woods

M. Butterfly

42nd Street

Dreamgirls

The Real Thing

Cats

Amadeus

La Cage aux Folles

Biloxi Blues

Anything Goes

Fool For Love

Les Miserables

Speed-the-Plow

Brighton Beach

The Phantom of the Opera

Glengarry Glen Ross

Big River

Song and Dance

CULTURE

1980s

Where Were You

1980

- The US boycotts the Summer Olympics in Moscow, to protest the Soviet invasion of Afghanistan
- Ronald Reagan is elected president
- Polish workers strike and Lech Walesa founds Solidarity
- Iran and Iraq begin to fight an eight-year war

1981

- The Iranian hostage crisis ends after 444 days
- The first space shuttle, the Columbia, is launched
- Pope John Paul II is shot and seriously wounded in Rome
- Egyptian president Anwar Sadat is assassinated in Cairo
- Air traffic controllers on strike are ordered back to work by President Reagan

1982

- The ERA is stopped three states short of ratification
- Argentina occupies the Falkland Islands, and Britain sends the navy to restore order
- Air Florida Flight 90 crashes on takeoff from Washington National Airport, landing in the Potomac River
- An economic recession hikes unemployment and drives many Americans into homelessness
- AT&T, the largest company in the world, is broken up by the US government

1983

- President Reagan proposes a space-based antiballistic missile system, coined Star Wars
- A truck bomb kills more than 200 US Marines in Beirut, Lebanon
- The US invades Grenada when Marxists take over the government in a bloody coup
- Lech Walesa wins the Nobel Peace Prize for his work with Solidarity
- First Lady Nancy's Reagan's "Just Say No" anti-drug campaign is launched
- In the Philippines, the opposition leader, Benigno Aquino, is assassinated
- A Soviet fighter downs a Korean civilian jet with 269 on board

1984

- Geraldine Ferraro is the first woman to run for vice president, with Walter Mondale
- President Reagan wins reelection in the largest Republican electoral vote landslide in history
- Leaking fumes kill over 2000 in Bhopal, India, in the world's worst industrial disaster
- Indira Gandhi is assassinated by her security guards

1985

- The wreck of the Titanic is discovered off the coast of Newfoundland
- A hole in the atmosphere's ozone layer is discovered over Antarctica
- Actor Rock Hudson dies of AIDS
- The cruise ship Achille Lauro is hijacked by Palestinian terrorists

When...?

1986

- The world's worst nuclear accident occurs at a power plant in Chernobyl, Ukraine, USSR
- The Supreme Court upholds affirmative action hiring quotas
- The Iran-Contra political scandal erupts and the Reagan administration is involved
- Dictator Ferdinand Marcos is deposed and flees the Philippines

1988

- Savings and loan institutions across the nation have overextended themselves, causing scandal and financial crisis
- Rev. Jesse Jackson makes a strong run for the Democratic presidential nomination
- Republicans George H. W. Bush and Dan Quayle are elected president and vice president

1987

- The Dow Jones Industrial Average drops 508 points on "Black Monday," the largest decline since 1914
- The US and Soviet Union sign the INF Treaty, eliminating all ground-launched intermediate-range nuclear missiles
- In Yugoslavia, Slobodan Milosevic seizes power and declares intent to restore Serbian dominance

1989

- Author Salman Rushdie is condemned to death by Iran's Ayatollah Khomeini, and goes into hiding
- The US invades Panama after General Manuel Noriega installs himself as president
- General Colin Powell is the first black American to become chairman of the Joint Chiefs of Staff
- In Beijing's Tiananmen Square, the Chinese army fires into a crowd of student demonstrators

The Buzz

Oliver North
Moral Majority
Rainbow Coalition
Glasnost
Baby Jessica
Margaret Thatcher
Family farm
Princess of Wales
Evil empire
Illegal immigrants
Hands Across America
Reaganomics
Homeless
Crack
AIDS
Supply-side economics
Prolife
Mikhail Gorbachev
Acid rain
Operation Abscam
Leona Helmsley
James Watt
Desmond Tutu
Junk bonds

HISTORY

1980s

12

WHAT WE WORE

Skinny ties
Designer jeans
Stirrup pants
medical scrubs
Rolex® watches
Bolero jackets
Polo® shirts
Power suits   Slipper shoes with bows
headbands   Hair mousse   Leg warmers
Slouch socks   Jeans with holes in the knees
Down vests   Izod® shirts
high top sneakers
Doc Martens®
Ponytails on the side
Swatch® watches
Tapered leg jeans, often
with a zipper in the leg
Prairie skirts   T-shirts tied on the side
with cowboy boots
Acid wash jeans   The mullet hairstyle
UNITS® clothing for women
Painter pants
Military
Rat tail haircut   fatigue pants
Hooded shirts
Shoulder pads   Bicycle shorts

The Buzz

- Calvin Klein®
- Brooke Shields
- Christie Brinkley
- Velour
- The mall
- Jellies®
- fitness
- Miami Vice look
- Cabbage Patch Kids®
- Punk
- Burberry®
- Banana clips
- Electric blue
- Fanny pack
- L.L.Bean®
- Valley Girl
- Beemer
- Wannabe
- Donkey Kong®
- Big hair

Popular Vacation Destinations

- Gulf of Mexico
- Cozumel, Mexico
- Cancun, Mexico
- Las Vegas, Nevada
- Myrtle Beach, South Carolina
- Virgin Islands
- The Rockies, Colorado

If You Had Wheels You Had to Drive a . . .

- Chrysler® minivan
- Ford Taurus®
- Honda Acura®
- Mazda Miata®
- BMW®
- Mercedes®
- Chevy Camaro®

Ben & Jerry's®
Ice Cream

Chipwich®
NutraSweet®
Latté   Espresso
Microwave pizza
New Coke®   Lunchables®
Sushi   Fresca®
Fruit Roll-ups®
Drink boxes
Almost Home cookies®   Diet Coke®
Bottled water   Perrier®
Fruit Roll-ups®   Breakfast burritos
Rice cakes   Lipton Cup-A-Soup®
Balsamic vinegar   Tex-Mex
Baked garlic
Blackened redfish
Bartles & Jaymes® wine coolers
Gourmet pizza

Food
Trends

Slush
Puppy®

Blackened Seasoning

3/4 tsp. onion powder

3/4 tsp. garlic powder

3/4 tsp. white pepper, ground

3/4 tsp. cayenne pepper, ground

3/4 tsp. black pepper, ground

3/4 tsp. teaspoon thyme, crushed

1/4 tsp. salt

Seasoning is enough for four fillets of fish, chicken, or beef. Brush with melted butter, then with spices. Grill in pan or over coals.

WHO WON?
THE WORLD SERIES

1980 ....Philadelphia Phillies 4, Kansas City Royals 2
1981 ....Los Angeles Dodgers 4, New York Yankees 2
1982 ....St. Louis Cardinals 4, Milwaukee Brewers 3
1983 ....Baltimore Orioles 4, Philadelphia Phillies 1
1984 ....Detroit Tigers 4, San Diego Padres 1
1985 ....Kansas City Royals 4, St. Louis Cardinals 3
1986 ....New York Mets 4, Boston Red Sox 3
1987 ....Minnesota Twins 4, St. Louis Cardinals 3
1988 ....Los Angeles Dodgers 4, Oakland Athletics 1
1989 ....Oakland Athletics 4, San Francisco Giants 0

WHO WON?
THE STANLEY CUP

1980 ....New York Islanders 4, Philadelphia Flyers 2
1981 ....New York Islanders 4, Minnesota North Stars 1
1982 ....New York Islanders 4, Vancouver Canucks 0
1983 ....New York Islanders 4, Edmonton Oilers 0
1984 ....Edmonton Oilers 4, New York Islanders 1
1985 ....Edmonton Oilers 4, Philadelphia Flyers 1
1986 ....Montreal Canadiens 4, Calgary Flames 1
1987 ....Edmonton Oilers 4, Philadelphia Flyers 3
1988 ....Edmonton Oilers 4, Boston Bruins 0
1989 ....Calgary Flames 4, Montreal Canadiens 2

THE NBA CHAMPIONSHIP

1980
Los Angeles Lakers 4
Philadelphia 76ers 2

1981
Boston Celtics 4
Houston Rockets 2

1982
Los Angeles Lakers 4
Philadelphia 76ers 2

1983
Philadelphia 76ers 4
Los Angeles Lakers 0

1984
Boston Celtics 4
Los Angeles Lakers 3

1985
Los Angeles Lakers 4
Boston Celtics 2

1986
Boston Celtics 4
Houston Rockets 2

1987
Los Angeles Lakers 4
Boston Celtics 2

1988
Los Angeles Lakers 4
Detroit Pistons 3

1989
Detroit Pistons 4
Los Angeles Lakers 0

THE SUPERBOWL

1980 .... Pittsburgh Steelers 31, Los Angeles Rams 19

1981 .... Oakland Raiders 27, Philadelphia Eagles 10

1982.. San Francisco 49ers 26, Cincinnati Bengals 21

1983.. Washington Redskins 27, Miami Dolphins 17

1984...................................... Los Angeles Raiders 38, Washington Redskins 9

1985.. San Francisco 49ers 38, Miami Dolphins 16

1986 .... Chicago Bears 46, New England Patriots 10

1987 .... New York Giants 39, Denver Broncos 20

1988.. Washington Redskins 42, Denver Broncos 10

1989 .... San Francisco 49ers 20, Cincinnati Bengals 16

The Buzz

FloJo
Jackie Joyner-Kersee
Athletic endorsements
George Brett
John Elway
Charlie Hustle
Jim Palmer
Michael Jordan
Zola Budd
Carl Lewis
Jim Kelly
Boris Becker
Sugar Ray Leonard
John McEnroe
Wayne Gretzky
Mary Lou Retton
Martina Navratilova
Miracle on Ice
Walter Payton
Greg Louganis
The No Más Fight
Joe Montana
Jerry Rice
The Great One
Dan Marino
Phil Mahre
Scott Hamilton
Magic Johnson

1980
- The Winter Olympics are held in Lake Placid, New York
- The US hockey team upsets the heavily-favored USSR on its way to winning a gold medal
- Eric Heiden wins every speed skating gold medal, from 500 meters to 10,000 meters
- The Summer Games are held in Moscow, USSR; the US boycotts

1981
- John Henry becomes the first horse to win a million dollar race at Arlington Park, in Chicago, Illinois
- United States wins 18 $\frac{1}{2}$ to 9 $\frac{1}{2}$ over Europe in world team golf Ryder Cup

1982
- Tom Watson chips in a spectacular birdie on the 17th hole at Pebble Beach, and snatches the US Open from Jack Nicklaus
- First regular season strike by NFL players ends on November 16th after 57 days

1983
- In a highly anticipated bout, Marvin Hagler retains his world Middleweight title with a unanimous decision over Roberto Duran
- In America's Cup yacht racing, Australia defeated the United States (skipper Dennis Conner), the first time in 132 years the US had not held the Cup
- Paul "Bear" Bryant, college football coach at the University of Alabama, dies

1984
- In retaliation for the US boycott, the USSR and the Eastern Bloc nations do not attend the Summer Olympics in Los Angeles, California
- Winter Olympics are held in Sarajevo, Yugoslavia

1985
- Pete Rose breaks Ty Cobb's 57-year-old record for most hits in a career
- Michael Jordan is named NBA Rookie of the Year
- Libby Riddles, with her lead dogs Axle and Dugan, is the first woman to ever win the Iditarod Trail Sled Dog Race

1986
- College basketball star Len Bias dies of a heart attack caused by a single use of cocaine
- Greg LeMond becomes the first American to win the Tour de France
- Boxer Mike Tyson is the youngest heavyweight champion ever
- In World Cup soccer, Argentina wins 3-2 over West Germany, in Mexico

1987
- Violations of recruiting regulations at Southern Methodist University are so egregious that its football season is canceled
- Dean Paul Martin (son of singer Dean Martin) 29, a tennis pro, is killed in plane crash

1988
- US swimmers Matt Biondi and Janet Evans are standouts at the Summer Olympics in Seoul, South Korea
- The first-ever night game at Wrigley Field is played
- Steffi Graf becomes only the third woman in history to win the Grand Slam in tennis: Wimbledon, the US Open, the French Open, and the Australian Open
- The Winter Olympic Games are held in Calgary, Alberta, Canada

1989
- Nolan Ryan of the Texas Rangers is the first pitcher in major league history to strike out 5,000 batters
- Pete Rose is banned from baseball (and from the Hall of Fame) for betting on major league games
- The US soccer team earns a berth in the final round of the World Cup for the first time since 1950
- The California earthquake delays the start of baseball's World Series by ten days

Life Just Wouldn't Be the Same Without...

Post-it Notes®
Sony® Watchman
Cordless phones
IBM® personal computer
Computer mouse
Lotus® 1-2-3 software
CD-ROMs/CDs
Microsoft®'s MS-DOS
Cellular phone network
Apple® Macintosh computer
Desktop laser printers
Microsoft® Windows
DNA sequencing
Disposable contact lenses
Digital audiotape
Rogaine® hair restorative
Nintendo® entertainment system
Disposable cameras

The Buzz

E-mail

Doppler radar

Flying Toasters

Product-tampering

Prozac®   Nicorette®

Pac-Man®   Floppy disk

Rubik's Cube®

Rollerblades®

Checklist for the Perfect Party

THREE WEEKS BEFORE:

- ☐ Plan the occasion > *an 80s nostalgia party*   ☐ Create a compatible guest list
- ☐ Choose a location that will accommodate the number of guests
- ☐ Send invitations [date, time (start/end), place, directions] > *Ask guests to dress in clothing of the era*
- ☐ Plan and select decorations > *This can include old yearbooks, record albums and other memorabilia*
- ☐ Begin collecting materials and creating props
  > *Movie memorabilia stores are good sources*
- ☐ Prepare menu and grocery list > *Consider using food from the era for extra nostalgia*
- ☐ Select and hire caterer/serving help (if using)

A FEW DAYS BEFORE:

- ☐ Call any guests who have not responded   ☐ Buy groceries and beverages
- ☐ Prepare and refrigerate/freeze food items that can be made in advance
- ☐ Make party costume or select outfit

ONE DAY BEFORE:

- ☐ Clean house, party room facility or other party site   ☐ Set up and arrange party room
- ☐ Thaw out frozen party foods   ☐ Get out serving pieces
- ☐ Coordinate last-minute arrangements with caterer, servers (if using)

THE DAY OF:

- ☐ Decorate party room   ☐ Prepare and arrange remaining food
- ☐ Coordinate set-up, service, cleanup with hired helpers (if using)
- ☐ Mentally travel through party > *BEGINNING: arrivals and introductions* > *MIDDLE: food and activities; have everyone sign the book* > *END: wrap it up! Party favors, disposable cameras*
- ☐ Dress in party outfit   ☐ Await guests
- ☐ Have a good time!

Happy Day!

Hope You Enjoyed Your Party... We Sure Did!

Celebrating You and the 1980s
©2004 Elm Hill Books
ISBN: 1404184724

For additions, deletions, corrections or clarifications in future editions of this text, please contact Paul Shepherd, Senior Acquisitions and Development Editor for Elm Hill Books.

Manuscript written and compiled by Jamie Chavez.

Layout and design created by Susan Rae Stegall of D/SR Design, LLC.

WE HEART HARRY

WE HEART HARRY

WE HEART HARRY

WE HEART

50 REASONS YOUR DREAM BOYFRIEND

HARRY STYLES IS PERFECTION

HARRY

Smith
Street
Books

WE HEART

50 REASONS YOUR DREAM BOYFRIEND

HARRY STYLES IS PERFECTION

HARRY

Harry was only 16 when he auditioned for The X Factor, singing Stevie Wonder's "ISN'T SHE LOVELY" a capella.

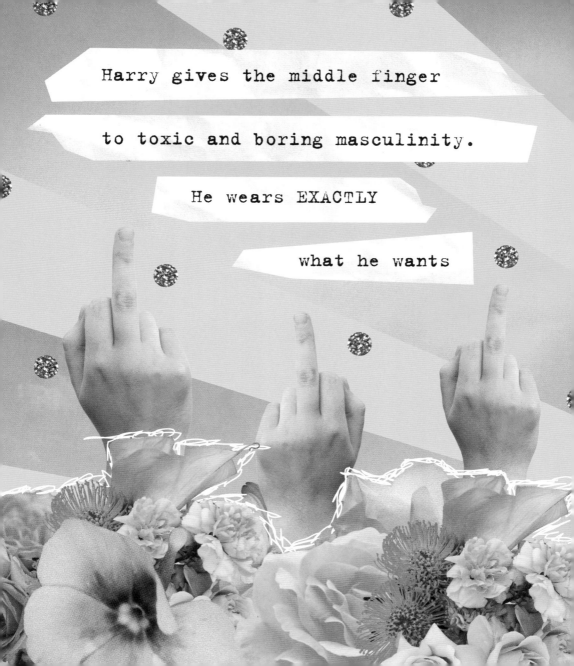

AND LOOKS...

FABULOUSSS.

As an after-school job, Harry slung pastries at W. Mandeville Bakery.

His former boss said that "He was the most polite member of staff we've ever had."

iS ANYONE EVEN SURPRiSED?

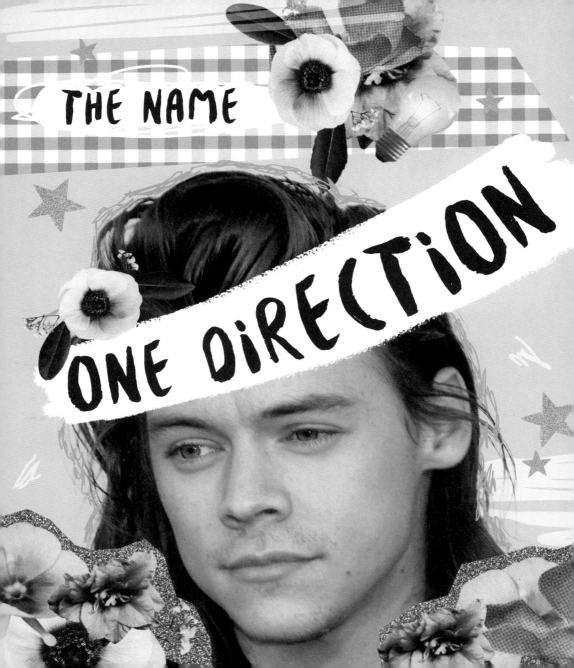

THE NAME

ONE DiRECTiON

WAS HARRY'S IDEA.

With those two words,
he changed the direction
of pop music history

FOREVER.

Harry is unabashedly schmaltzy.

He loves romcoms and his favorite films are tear-jerkers — The Notebook, Love Actually, and Titanic.

PASS THE TISSUES,

PLEASE.

He's an

AQUARIUS.

As a fellow air sign, that makes us a perfect

COSMIC MATCH.

(JUST SAYIN...)

One Direction never won
The X Factor.

Instead,

they came third

and proceeded to casually take over

THE WORLD,

becoming one of the best-selling

boy bands

OF ALL TIME.

Growing up, Harry had a pet hamster.

In a sign of the creativity that would make him into a MEGASTAR, HARRY NAMED IT... HAMSTER.

WHEN HARRY WAS

15,

he spent nearly all his after-school wages on long train trips to visit his first girlfriend.

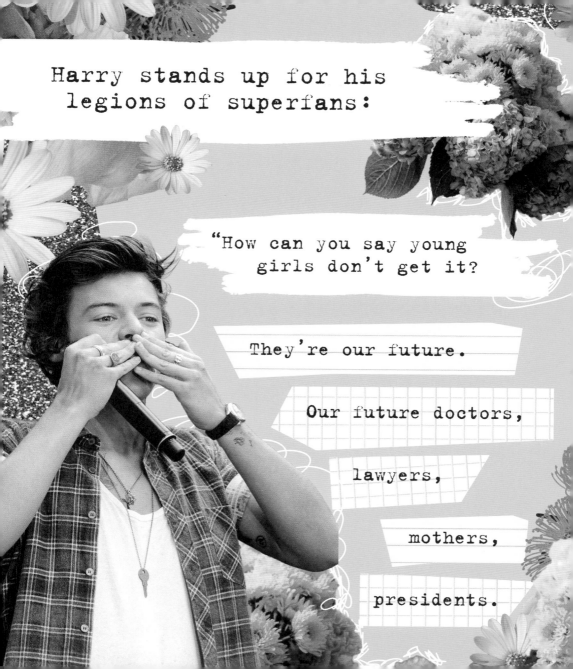

Harry stands up for his legions of superfans:

"How can you say young girls don't get it?

They're our future.

Our future doctors,

lawyers,

mothers,

presidents.

They kind of keep the world going."

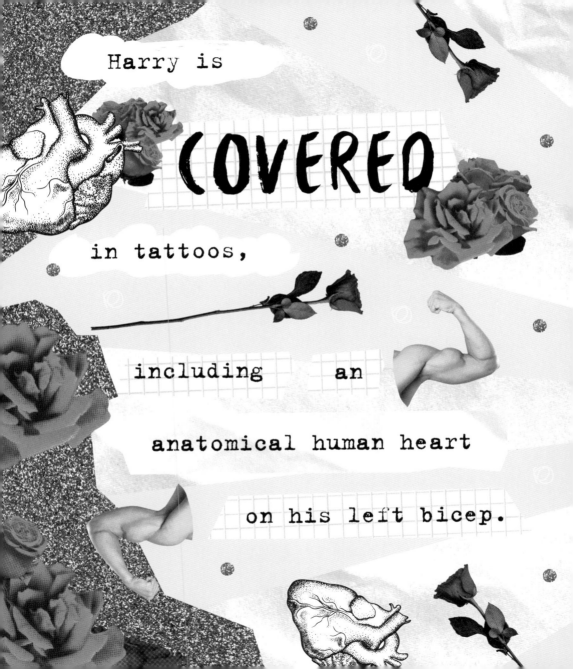

Harry is

COVERED

in tattoos,

including an

anatomical human heart

on his left bicep.

He literally wears his heart

on his sleeve.

When Harry first joined Instagram, his handle was

@GIVEMEMYNAMEPLEASE

as a cheeky

protest until the owner of

@harrystyles finally

handed over the reins.

Harry and Lizzo are OBSESSED with each other.

Nothing is more **iCONiC** than the footage of "Hizzo" flirting and giggling over **TEQUiLA** at the 2020 Brit Awards.

He made his

acting debut in

CHRISTOPHER

NOLAN'S

adrenaline-fueled **DUNKIRK,** looking damn **FINE** in a uniform.

HARRY'S PARTIAL TO VINTAGE CARS.

He can take us for a ride around London in his primrose yellow '73 Jaguar

ANY TIME.

Harry bought a new mattress to celebrate

"Up All Night" topping the US charts.

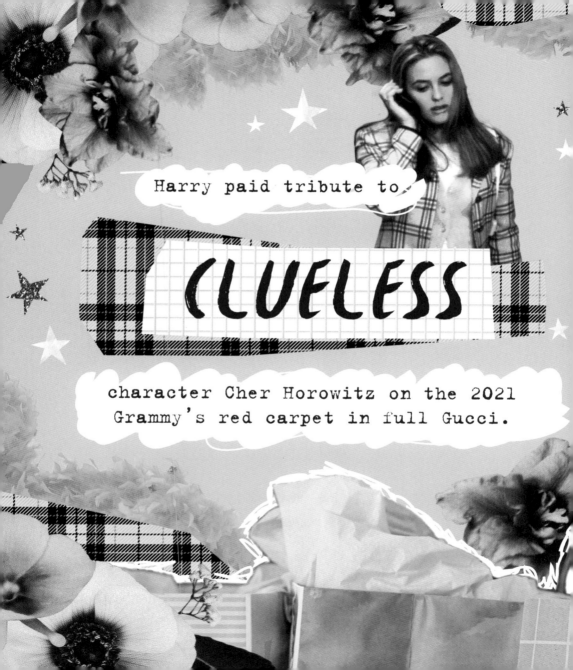

Harry paid tribute to

CLUELESS

character Cher Horowitz on the 2021
Grammy's red carpet in full Gucci.

From the plaid blazer to the
purple feather boa, this look
had the internet, like,

TOTALLY

BUGGiN!

Grammy? Yep. Brit Award? Sure. People's Choice Awards? Obvi.

Harry's surely tracking for

EGOT STATUS.

HARRY IS A   GENEROUS

KING!

Aside from his formal philanthropy, he used a day off in LA to buy and hand deliver $3000 worth of pizza to the homeless.

ACCORDING

TO HIS SISTER,

Harry used to wear a

hand-me-down dalmatian outfit

an INORDINATE amount

of the time'.

Despite being one of

the **BIGGEST**

pop stars on the planet,

Harry used to get major stage fright. And somehow that makes him even CUTER.

His precious mum, Anne, was the one who submitted his *X-Factor* application.

CHEERS, MUM!

Harry really puts the

STYLE in HARRY STYLES.

He's risen to GOD-TIER status in the fashion world,

co-chairing the Met Gala in 2019 and becoming the first man to appear solo on a Vogue cover.

STEVIE NICKS

has been Harry's close friend
since they met backstage at a

FLEETWOOD MAC **CONCERT** in 2015.

It was Stevie's birthday, and Harry
appeared with a cake complete with
her name hand-piped on top.

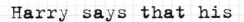

Harry says that his

FRIENDSHIPS

are the most

valuable thing

in his life.

CRYING EMOJI

Once, Harry's car broke down in front of a fan's house. She wasn't home (can you imagine???), but her dad let Harry in to use the phone.

Harry left her an adorable note and even fed her fish.

Harry has repeatedly cited

SHANIA TWAIN

as a huge

influence in both music

and fashion.

You might say that she

DOES, INDEED,

impress him much.

HE'S FUNNY.

Never was this more
evident than when Harry hosted
THE LATE LATE SHOW
the day James Cordon's
daughter was born.

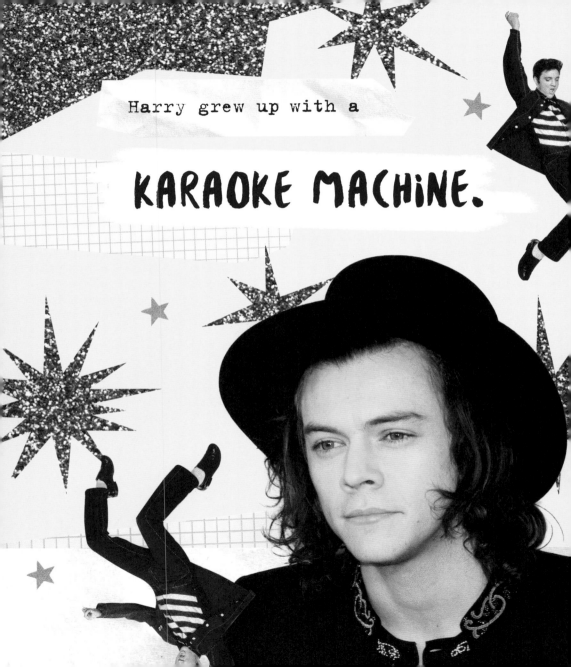

Harry grew up with a

KARAOKE MACHINE.

He'd entertain his grandparents with Elvis renditions, but his favorite track was always

"ENDLESS LOVE"

by Diana Ross and Lionel Richie.

"Watermelon Sugar" got the internet feelin'

HOT
AND
HEAVY,

with thirsty fans deciding

THE SONG'S LYRICS CELEBRATE

A CERTAIN

type of lovemaking.

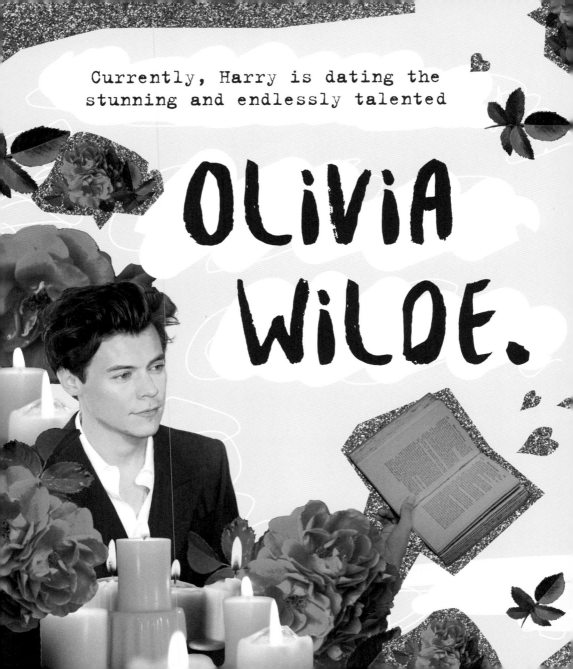

Currently, Harry is dating the stunning and endlessly talented

OLIVIA WILDE.

Together they are the power couple to end all power couples.

Harry's ever-

BLOSSOMING

solo career has defied

the trajectory

of most boy band alumni.

We stan a

well-mannered,

ENGLISH

GENTLEMAN.

Harry is famously punctual

and polite to

everyone he meets.

FOR ANYONE

who wants
to claim

he doesn't
have talent,

Harry can also juggle
and play the

KAZOO.

IN HIS

ONE DIRECTION DAYS,

the band recorded their albums on the road, in a van with no air conditioning.

Harry has worked (and sweated) for his fame.

Once, Harry managed to get a rare
picture beside a smiling Van Morrison.

Harry jokes that he got Van to crack a grin by tickling him on the back.

OH, TO BE THAT BACK.

On the set of the

"WATERMEL

ON SUGAR"

music video, Harry set a clear
standard of consent for physical contact
between the cast.

WE LOVE TO SEE IT!

Harry had to **CHOP OFF HIS** luxurious One Direction **LOCKS** to film *Dunkirk*.

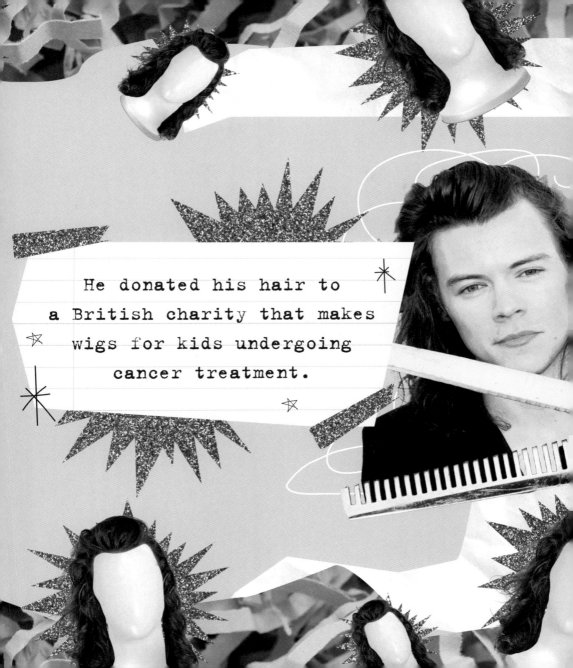

He donated his hair to a British charity that makes wigs for kids undergoing cancer treatment.

The intense online fandom surrounding Harry inspired the critically acclaimed (and stupidly funny) Australian musical Fangirls.

SO. DAMN.

WHOLESOME.

Harry's second solo album

FINE LINE

was included in Rolling Stone's "500 Greatest Albums

OF

ALL

TIME"

in 2020.

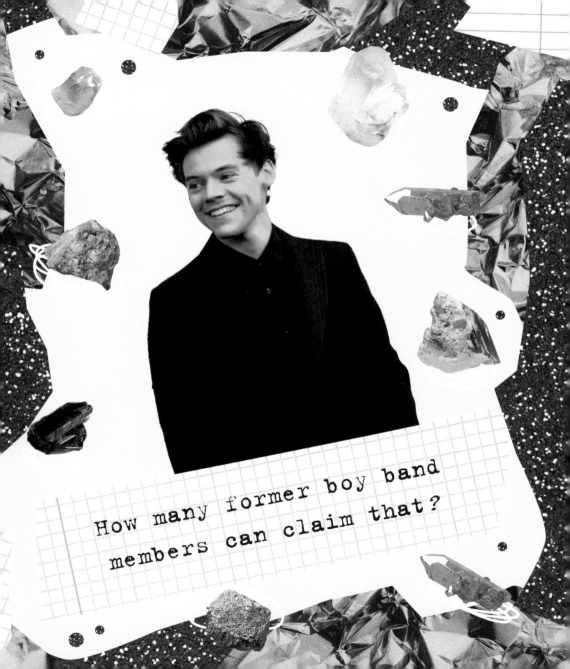

How many former boy band members can claim that?

His list of song writing credits includes tracks for

ARIANA GRANDE, MEGHAN TRAINOR AND MICHEAL BUBLÉ.

He's also collaborated with

TAYLOR SWIFT,

JOHN LEGEND,

AND

BRUNO MARS.

Harry says a school play might have kicked off his flair for fashion.

He played a church mouse named Barney and the costume included his first-ever pair of tights.

I'm sure the performance was moving.

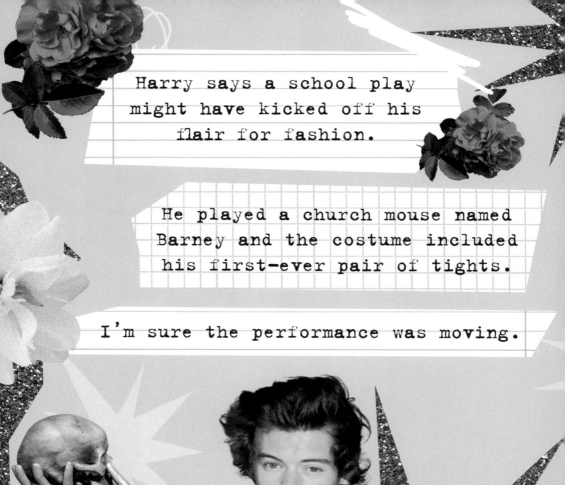

The following statement is
presented without comment:

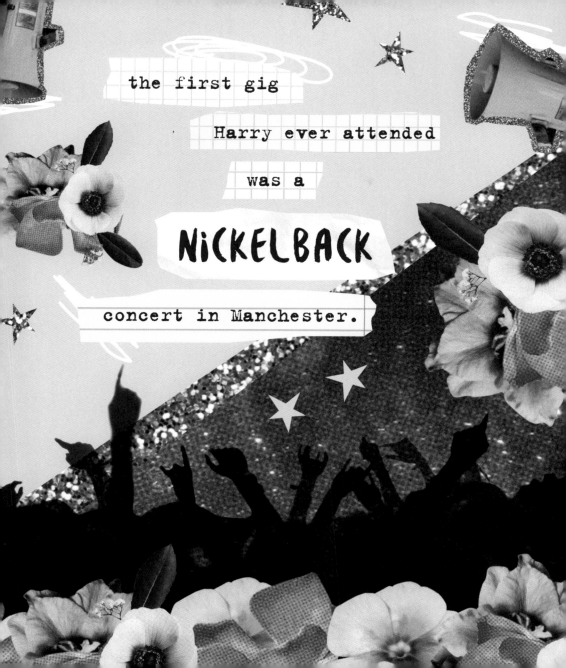

the first gig
Harry ever attended
was a

NICKELBACK

concert in Manchester.

Harry donated

a whopping

$1.2 M

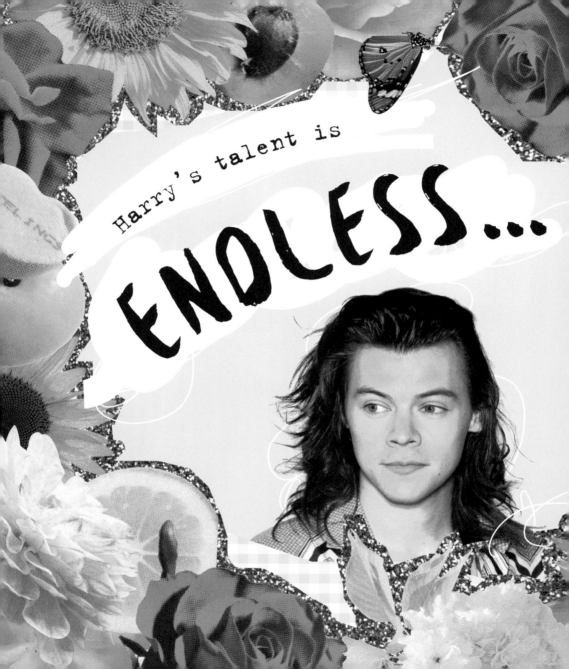

Harry's talent is

ENDLESS...

just like our love

for him.

Published in 2022 by Smith Street Books
Naarm | Melbourne | Australia
smithstreetbooks.com

ISBN: 978-1-92241-765-7

Publisher: Paul McNally
Project editor: Avery Hayes
Design and layout: George Saad & Emi Chiba
Proofreader: Hannah Koelmeyer

Printed & bound in China by C&C Offset Printing Co., Ltd.

Book 196
10 9 8 7 6 5 4 3 2 1